water

around

me

Created by Regina Wamba

Water Around Me: A Just Write Journal

Copyright 2017 © All rights reserved.

Cover design by Mae I Design & Photography

Book design by Regina Wamba & Inkstain Design Studio

water around me

goals
&
deadlines

writing
prompts

She touched the water and it glimmered like hope in an abyss of darkness....

The ocean was inside his soul, his mind, and he could no longer deny its call.

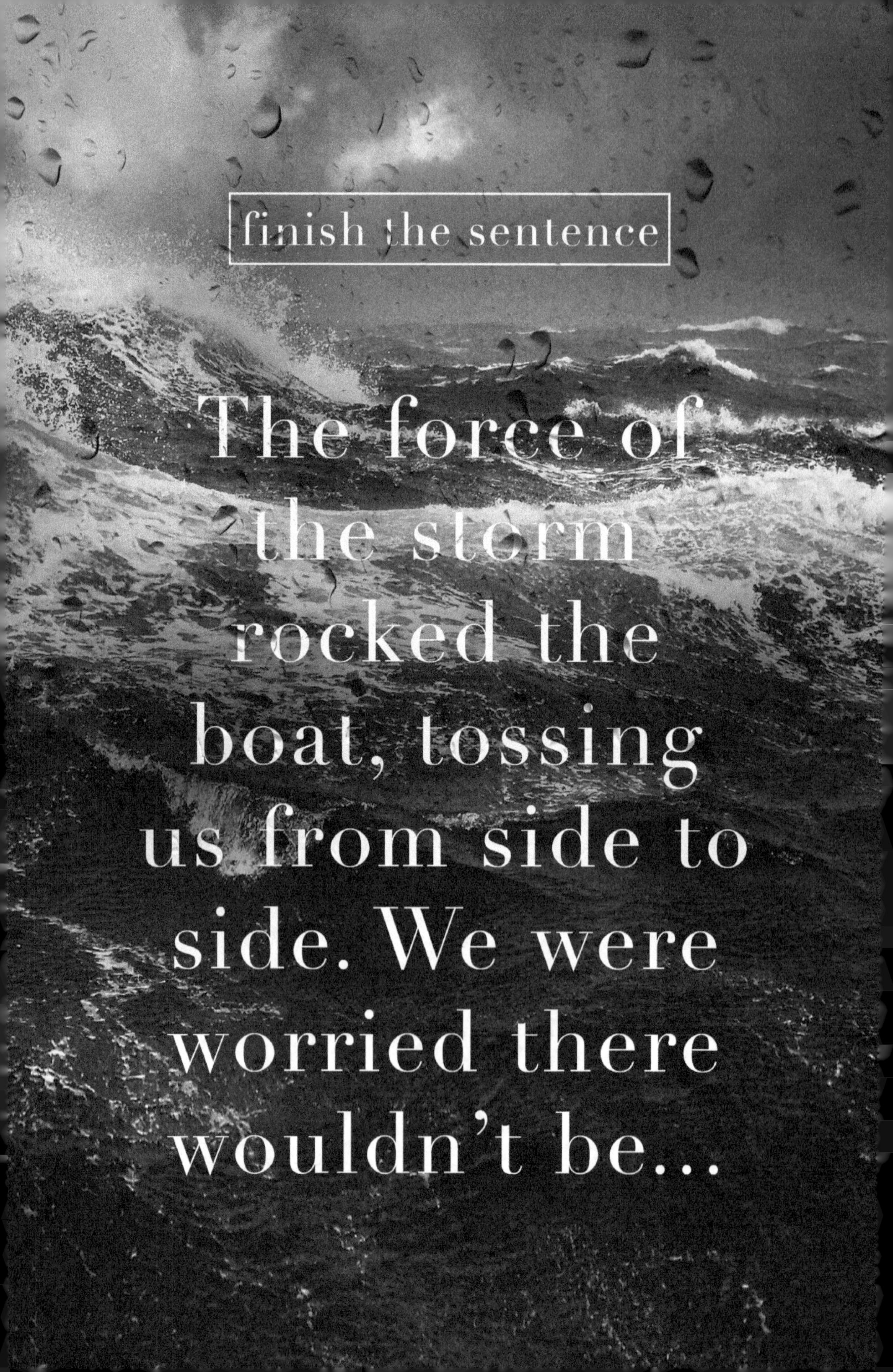

finish the sentence

The force of the storm rocked the boat, tossing us from side to side. We were worried there wouldn't be...

free

writing

vision board

write down your dreams
and aspirations, then
doodle/paste in images
that encapture them

writing prompts

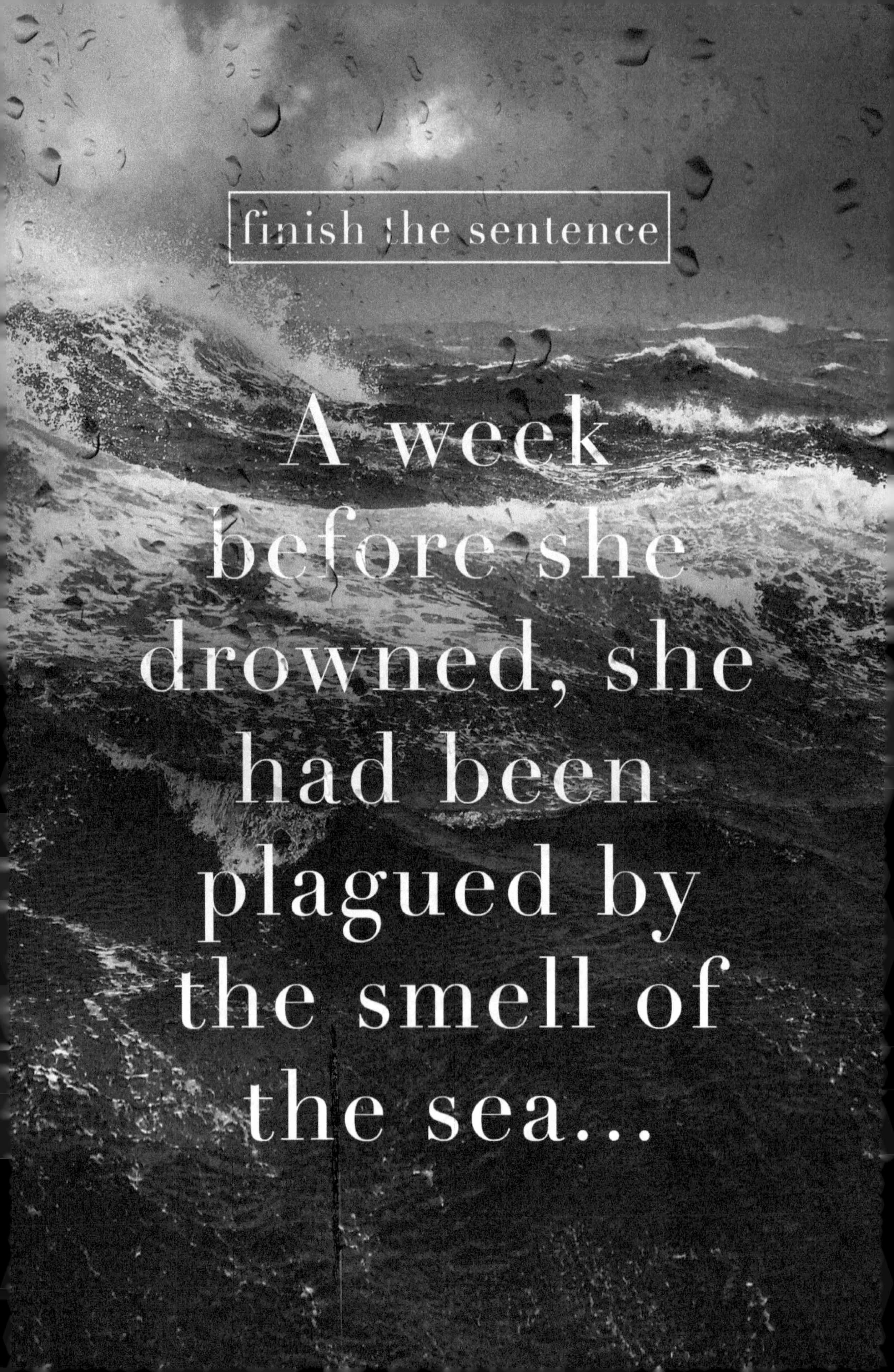

A week before she drowned, she had been plagued by the smell of the sea...

write the story

I was deep in the waters, lost to a place where light couldn't go and the mists consumed me.

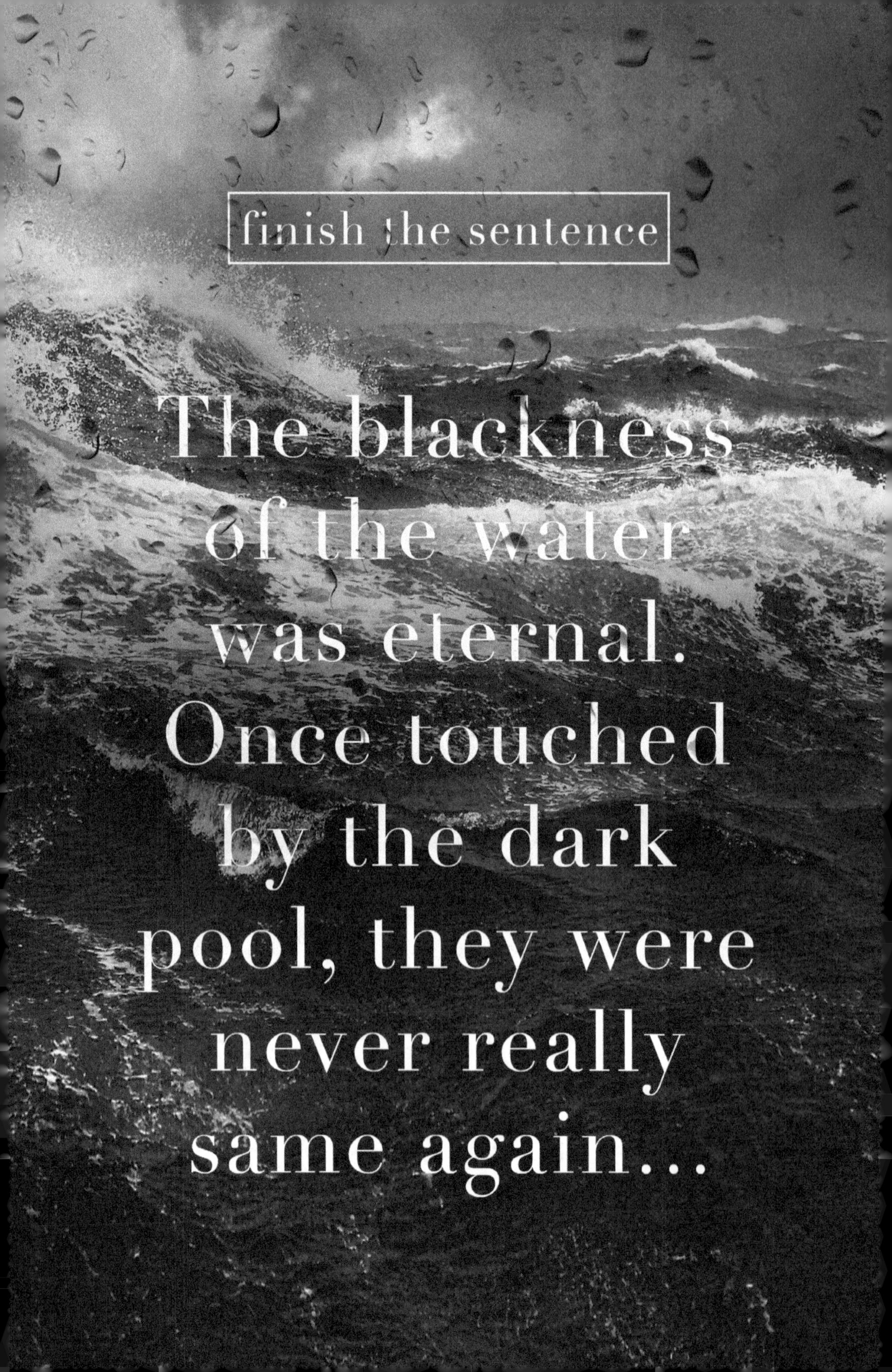
finish the sentence
The blackness of the water was eternal. Once touched by the dark pool, they were never really same again...

inspiring words

use these lists of words to
spark new story ideas

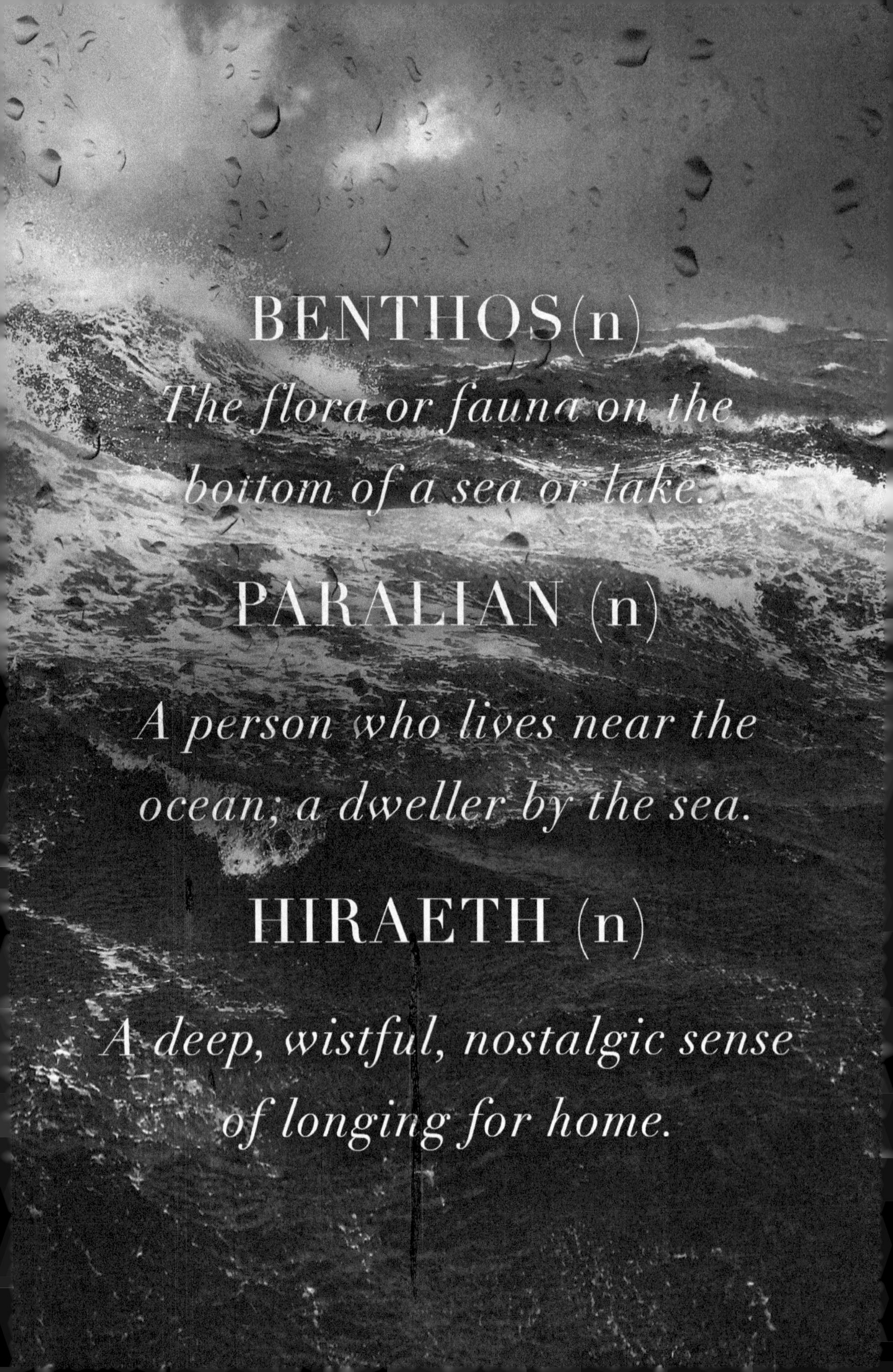

BENTHOS (n)

The flora or fauna on the bottom of a sea or lake.

PARALIAN (n)

A person who lives near the ocean; a dweller by the sea.

HIRAETH (n)

A deep, wistful, nostalgic sense of longing for home.

RECHERCHÉ (adj)

Carefully chosen; rare, exotic.

GIBIGIANNA (n)

*The play of light reflected
from water or a mirror.*

VAGARY (n)

*An unpredictable instance;
a wandering journey.*

black
space

about
the designer

I graduated in 2006 from Brown College with a Degree in Visual Communications (Graphic Design). In 2010, I joined a forum and started doing fan art, using my design to make art from the books I read. While there, I met authors and the idea of covers and self-published work snowballed into what I've built today.